This book is dedicated to Rachael, the most delightful grandchild imaginable.

Edited by Aileen Andres Sox
Designed by Dennis Ferree
Art by Mary Rumford
Typeset in 14/18 Weiss

ISBN: 0-8163-1124-2

98 99 00 01 02 ● 5 4 3 2

No Olives Tonight!

By Linda Porter Carlyle   **Illustrated by Mary Rumford**

Pacific Press® Publishing Association
Nampa, Idaho
Oshawa, Ontario, Canada

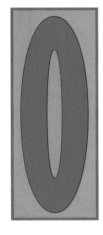h, no!" says Mama, looking at the elevator doors.

"What's the matter?" I ask her, peeking around the big bag in my arms.

"See that sign?" answers Mama. "It says 'Out of Service.' That means the elevator isn't working. We'll have to carry Aunt Minnie's groceries up the stairs."

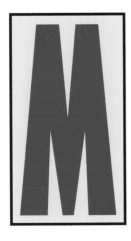**M**ama and I clump slowly up the stairway. Our arms are full of heavy, big brown bags. We climb all the way up to the third floor. Finally we stop in front of Aunt Minnie's door.

ama bends over to put the key into the lock. There is a tearing sound, and all the cans drop out of the bottom of one of Mama's bags. Some of them roll down the hallway. Some of them fall on Mama's feet.

I look at Mama. "I think your bag is out of service," I say.

Mama and I kiss Aunt Minnie goodbye. We go back down the stairs and outside to our car. It is almost night.

T he bank is closed already," says Mama. "But we can stop by the money machine outside the bank. I will cash my check, and we will pick up a pizza on the way home."

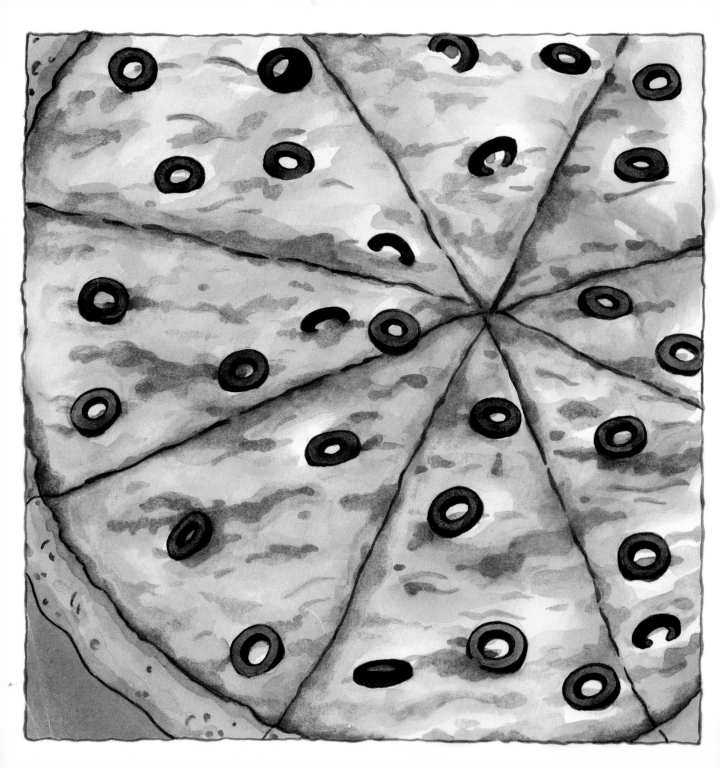

 buckle my seat belt and smile to myself in the darkness. Black olives. A pizza with lots of black olives. That's my favorite.

Mama stops the car by the curb in front of the bank. "Oh, no!" she says.

"hat's the matter?" I ask.

"See that sign on the money machine?" answers Mama. "It says 'Out of Service.'"

"Does that mean no pizza for supper?" I ask.

"I'm afraid so," says Mama. She steers our car back into the traffic. "I guess we will have soup."

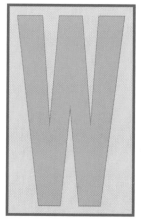e are quiet in the car. I am thinking. "I don't like it when things are out of service," I say.

"I know," agrees Mama, "but it's even worse when people are out of service."

"What do you mean?" I ask.

"Well," she says, "Jesus has a special job for us here on earth. He wants us to show His love to other people. And one way we can do that is by being of service. When we see someone who needs help, we help them."

e are home. I wiggle out of my coat. Mama disappears into the kitchen. She comes back and sits down on the couch. "I set the kitchen timer for twenty minutes," she says. "I need to take a little nap before I fix supper." She takes off her shoes and lies down. "Can you play quietly for a little while?" she asks.

I look at Mama on the couch. Her eyes are already shut. I am hungry. Mama is tired. I will be of service.

I go into the kitchen. I look around. I can't fix soup, but I can fix cereal. I put the cereal box on the table. I put two bowls and two spoons on the table. I take the jar of applesauce out of the refrigerator and put it on the table. I work very quietly.

n a few minutes, the timer will buzz. I will wake Mama up. She will be so surprised that supper is ready! I will tell her I am in service. She will give me a giant hug. I think Jesus would like to hug me too.

od, please help me work for You and show Your love to everyone.

I want to be of service forever.

Parent's Guide

Share the Joy of Helping Others With Your Child

When TJ's mother takes him with her to Aunt Minnie's, she is teaching him about the joy of helping others. Her joyful service teaches TJ by example. Here are some ideas to help you teach your child about service:

❖ Let your child hear you planning to do extra around the house to help a family member who is overworked or tired. Take over one of your child's chores from time to time, "just because I love you and wanted to help you."

❖ Be cheerful when you're helping others. Set an example of willing, happy service. Talk about the joy you get in helping others.

❖ Make birthdays and Christmas a time to give as well as receive gifts. Help your child plan special gifts for his family and friends. These gifts need not be elaborate, just thoughtful expressions of love. When your child gets a new toy for a special occasion, help her look through her things for a good used toy to share with a child who needs one. Make a family project out of giving away a Christmas box to a needy family.

❖ When you hear of someone in the community or church who needs help, involve your whole family in planning how to help and carrying out the plan.

❖ When it's time to shop for new clothing for your child, help her set aside clothing she has outgrown to give to someone else.

❖ Take pictures of your family doing service projects. Look through the albums from time to time and talk about the fun you had doing each project. Or, write about your projects in a family journal.

❖ Let your child hear you telling another adult about how proud you are of a specific time when he was especially helpful.

❖ Encourage your child to help others and sometimes keep it a secret. In this way, she will learn there is inner satisfaction in helping, even when she isn't thanked by the person she helped.

❖ The picture of Jesus tying TJ's shoe can start a discussion of how Jesus helped other people. Tell your child the story of Jesus washing His disciples' feet—a dirty job meant for a servant, done willingly and happily by the King of the universe.

Linda Porter Carlyle and Aileen Andres Sox

Books by Linda Porter Carlyle

I Can Choose
A Child's Steps to Jesus

God and Joseph and Me	*Cookies in the Mailbox*
Rescued From the River!	*Beautiful Bones and Butterflies*
Grandma Stepped on Fred!	*No Olives Tonight!*
Max Moves In	*Happy Birthday Tomorrow to Me!*